BE ON
GUARD
STAND FIRM
ON YOUR
FAITH

First edition: 2022

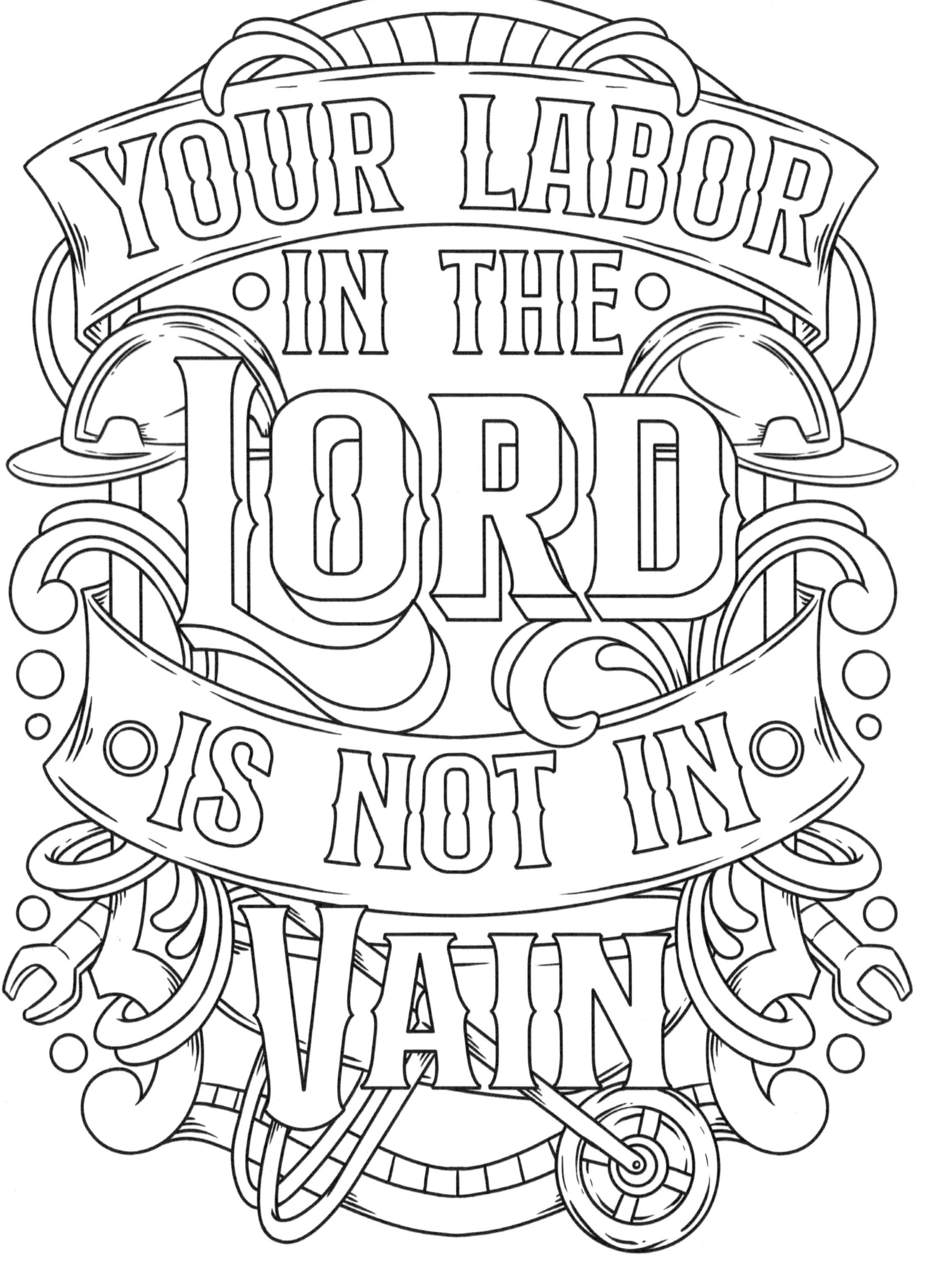
YOUR LABOR
IN THE
LORD
IS NOT IN
VAIN

I WILL
MAKE YOU
FISHERS
OF MEN

A MAN IS NOTHING WITHOUT GOD

MORE
OF HIM
LESS OF
ME

A MAN
SHOULD BE
QUICK TO
LISTEN
SLOW TO
SPEAK
SLOW TO
ANGER

GREATER
IS HE
WHO
LIVES
IN ME

CHILD
OF THE
ONE
TRUE
KING

JUST AN
ORDINARY
GUY
SAVED BY
GRACE

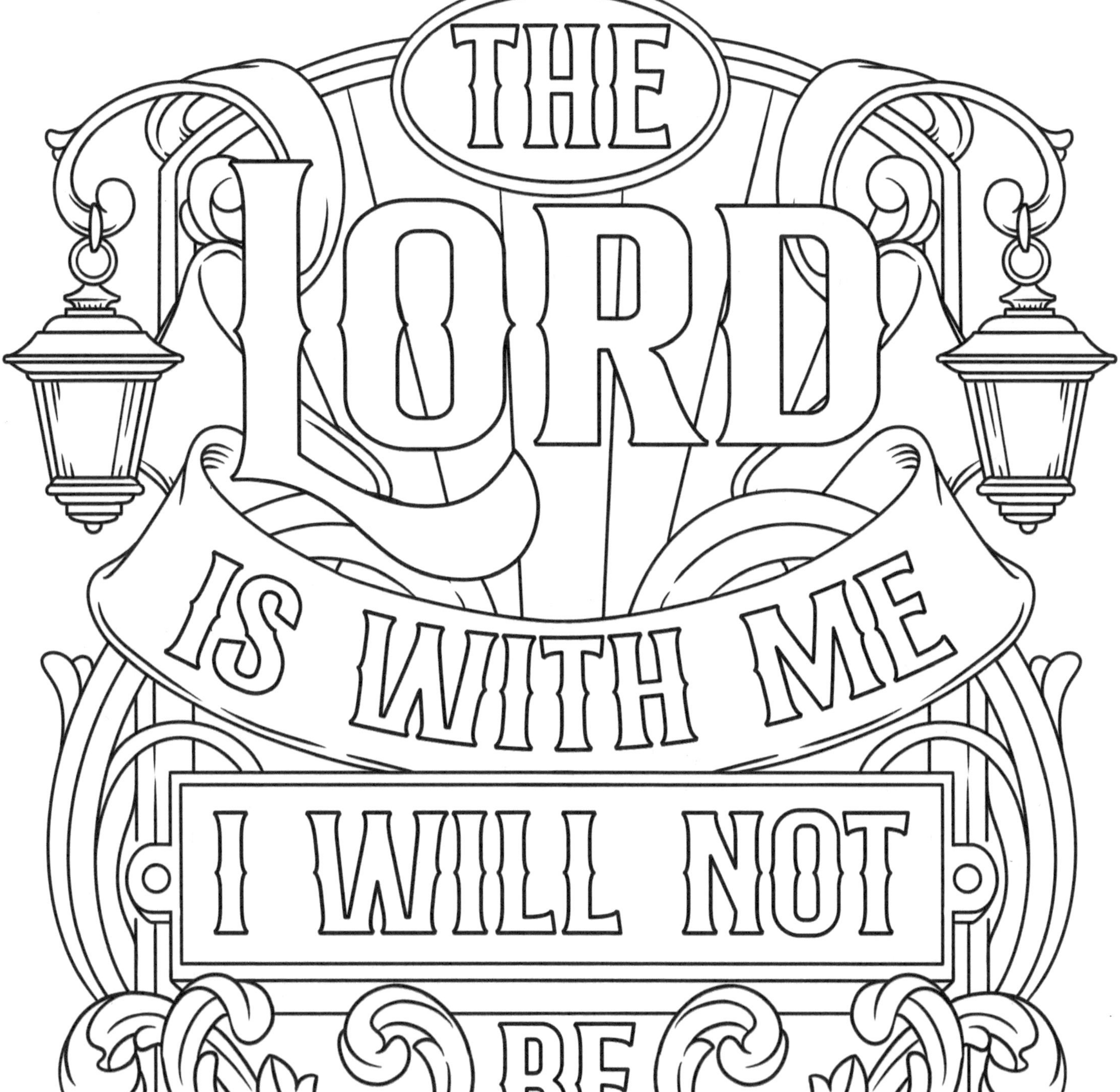
THE
LORD
IS WITH ME
I WILL NOT
BE
AFRAID

AS IRON SHARPENS IRON SO ONE MAN SHARPENS ANOTHER

DELIGHT
YOURSELF
IN THE
LORD

NO
GIANT
IS
GREATER
THAN
GOD

LET YOUR
LIGHT
SHINE
BEFORE
MEN

MEN
PLANS
GOD
DECIDES

HE WHO
KNEELS
BEFORE
GOD CAN
STAND
BEFORE
ANYONE

A WISE
MAN
FEARS
THE LORD

THE LORD IS MY SHEPHERD I SHALL NOT WANT

WALK
HUMBLY
BEFORE
GOD

DENYING
THE
WORLD
OBEYING
HIS
WORD

WITH
MAN
IT'S
IMPOSSIBLE
BUT NOT
WITH
GOD

IF THE
LORD
DELIGHTS
IN A MAN'S
WAY
HE MAKES HIS
STEPS
FIRM

I WILL
INSTRUCT
YOU
AND TEACH YOU
IN THE WAY
YOU
SHOULD
GO

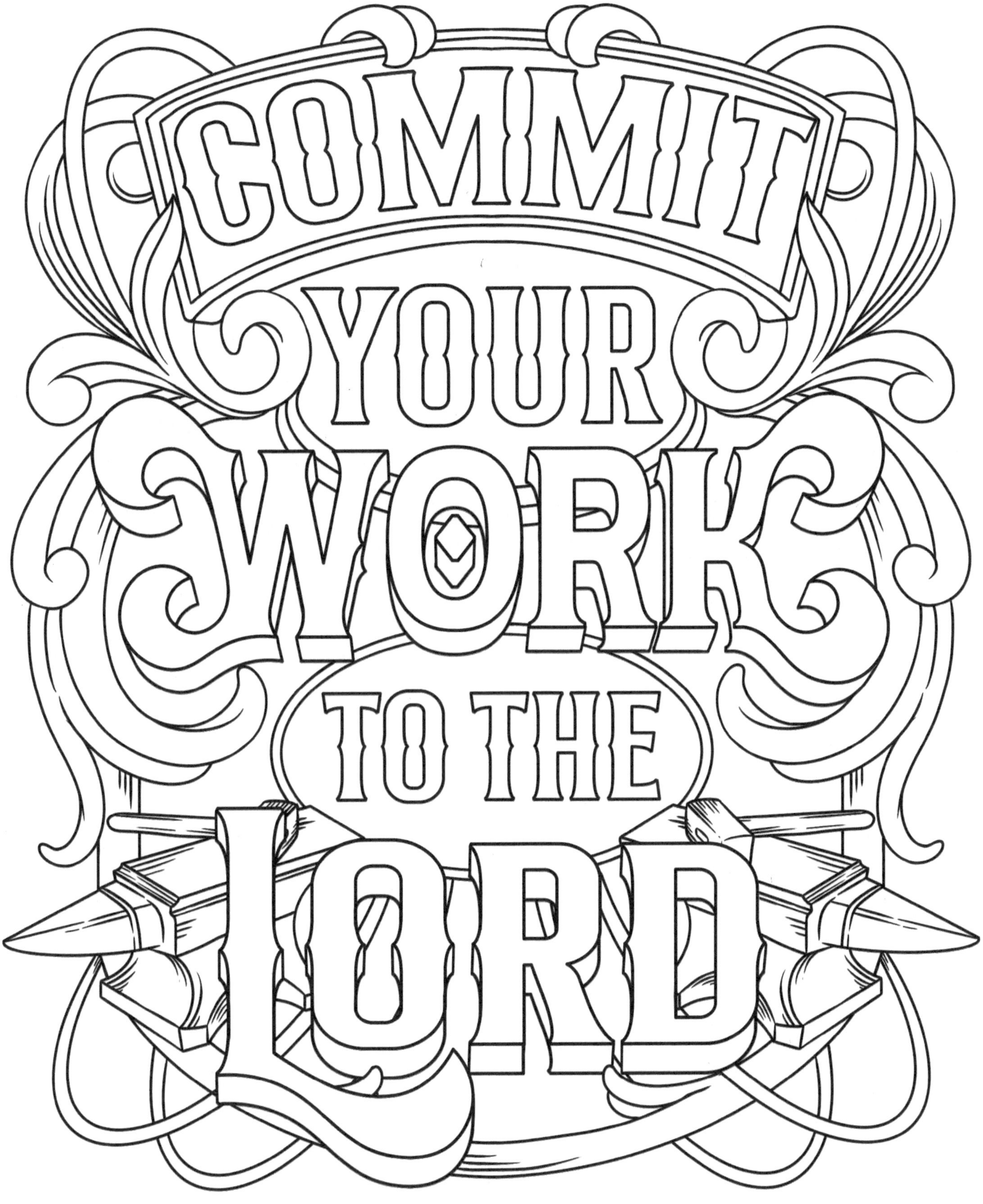
COMMIT
YOUR
WORK
TO THE
LORD

BLESSED
IS THE
MAN
WHO
REVERES
GOD

Made in United States
Troutdale, OR
11/15/2024

24835470R00031